Opus Alchymicum

J. Daniel Gunther

WENNOFER HOUSE

Opus Alchymicum

An Illuminated Epistle on the Stone of the Philosophers
The Black Edition
Edited and Translated for Study

Christ of the World

I parried savage, hardy thorns
    huddled thick and wild
where footpaths seldom lead; so dense
    the morning breath evoking dew
was stagnant, left from bygone days.
The latter mist of sunrise past
    had failed to filter through the rough
where tangled weed and creeping vine
    defied their thirst and held to life
with mad, tenacious grip. And I,
    though the miscreant,
pushed on as driven, searching deep
    within the ill-known chaparral
for sign of He who passed before;
    of whom the braver prophet wrote,
had a blood red Rose in mystic
    bloom upon the aureate Rood.
Emblazoned on a flag unfurled
    this signet crest and sacred shield
hails Christ of the World.

And with such word and greater hope
　　I pressed beyond the rugged land
where thickets bar the finer way
　　and tear resolve to tattered fear.
No clearing found my patient trail
　　and sterner still the mountain peak
that lifted up above the wood,
　　its crown but glimmers in the cloud
blotting out the sky.
　　With halting nerve my weary feet
engrafted hold upon the stone.
My march caught up the languid flesh,
　　propelled me onward to that height
that mortals call empyrean
　　where, in my dream, the heavens hurled
the lighting spears that guard the door
　　to Christ of the World

J. Daniel Gunther

An epistle from Eugnostos the blessed to his beloved son concerning the Opus Alchymicum:

My beloved son, I begin my discourse by imparting unto you these words, preserved by Stobaeus of Macedonia in his Anthologium:

Ἑπτὰ πολυπλανέες κατ' Ὀλύμπιον ἀστέρες οὐδὸν
εἰλεῦνται, μετὰ τοῖσι δ' ἀεὶ περινίσσεται αἰών·
νυκτιφανὴς Μήνη, στυγνὸς Κρόνος, Ἥλιος ἡδύς,
παστοφόρος Παφίη, θρασὺς Ἄρης, εὔπτερος Ἑρμῆς,
καὶ Ζεὺς ἀρχιγένεθλος, ἀφ' οὗ φύσις ἐβλάστησεν.
Οἱ δ' αὐτοὶ μερόπων ἔλαχον γένος, ἔστι δ' ἐν ἡμῖν
Μήνη, Ζεύς, Ἄρης, Παφίη, Κρόνος, Ἥλιος, Ἑρμῆς·
Τοὔνεκ' ἀπ' αἰθερίου μεμερίσμεθα πνεύματος ἕλκειν
δάκρυ, γέλωτα, χόλον, γένεσιν, λόγον, ὕπνον, ὄρεξιν.
Δάκρυ μέν ἐστι Κρόνος, Ζεὺς δ' ἡ γένεσις, λόγος Ἑρμῆς,
θυμὸς Ἄρης, Μήνη δ' ἄρ' ὕπνος, Κυθέρεια δ' ὄρεξις,
Ἥλιός τε γέλως· τούτῳ γὰρ ἅπασα δικαίως
καὶ θνητὴ διάνοια γελᾷ καὶ κόσμος ἀπείρων.

There are seven wandering stars that revolve about the threshold of Olympus, and moving among them, Eternity circles forever.

The Moon shining by night, somber Saturn, the joyful Sun, the shrine of Venus, bold Mars, wingéd Mercury, and Jupiter the progenitor who did not spring forth from nature.

To these same stars the human race is assigned and we have within us the Moon ☽, Jupiter ♃, Mars ♂, Venus ♀, Saturn ♄, the Sun ☉ and Mercury ☿.

Therefore, it is our destiny to breathe in the Spirit of the Æthyr ⊕, tears, laughter, anger, birth, speech, sleep and desire.

Tears most certainly are Saturn, Jupiter is birth, speech is Mercury, the temper Mars, the Moon sleep, Venus is desire, the Sun is laughter; for by him laugh all well-balanced men, mortal Reason and the boundless Cosmos.

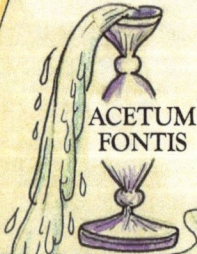

OPUS ALCHYMICUM

figure 1

Behold the nature of our Work, which previously I declared unto you speaking of the Holy Marriage of the LION and EAGLE.

Now I reveal to you that they are also known unto us as the Black King and the White Queen; or further, as Yod and Heh, Fire and Water, Lance and Cup, Gold and Silver. And in Ruach Elohim are they united and the Holy Spirit bestows Grace upon the Child of their union, the Divine Hermaphrodite, who is at once the Christ, Mercurius, the Spirit of the Aethyr, the Logos, the Savior of the world. As it is written, "In the beginning was the Word and the Word was with God, and the Word was God". For Yod united with Heh produces Vau the Son whose Nature is threefold, having the aspect of the Father, the Mother and the Holy Spirit. Know therefore, that it is our destiny to breathe in the Spirit of the Aethyr.

Amen

IGNE NATURA RENOVATUR INTEGRA

אש   מים   דם

DONUM SPIRITUS SANCTI

פרי   עץ

PRIMA   MATERIA

גולגלתא

LAPIS NOSTER HIC EST IGNIS EX IGNE CREATUS ET IN IGNUM VERTITUR,
ET ANIMA EIUS IN IGNE MORATUR.

figure 2

Lo, I give you a Key to the nature of our Work, the quest for the Stone of the Philosophers. It proceedeth as Adam, the first man, out of the original substance of non-existence which some call the first Death, to become the Sun, the Heavenly Fire. And as the Sun perishes in the North on the Great Cross during the Time of Capricornus, so must he be crucified on the Fourfold Cross of the Universe, the Tree of Life. And this is the second Death which takes place at Golgotha, which is to say, "the Place of the Skull." Upon death he relinquishes his threefold aspect which his Name in Hebrew conceals; Fire, Blood and Water; אש דם מים; This is the gift of the Holy Spirit that waters the fruit of the Tree and renews the fruit of the Tree. And over his head is placed the writing INRI, signifying that the whole of Nature is renewed by Fire. For our Stone is Fire; created of Fire and turns into Fire. Its Soul dwells in Fire.

אדם

στρογγύλος καὶ τετράγωνος

DIVIDE LAPIDEM TUUM IN QUATUOR ELEMENTA
ET CONIUNGE IN UNUM ET TOTUM HABEBIS MAGISTERIUM

figure 3

Our Stone dwells within the Heart of Man which is also called the Garden of Eden. Adam, the three (אדם) which is Four (A△AM), the round who is square, is crucified on the Cross of the four rivers flowing outward from Eden; Pison, Gihon, Hiddakel and Phrath. For the heart or center of Man, that is אדם, is the letter ד which has the value of 4. And the 4 rivers of Eden go into Havilah where there is Gold. Know from this that you must reduce the Stone into 4 elements, and unite it again into One. This, they say, is the whole of the Magistry.

יוד
יהוה

לא המטיר
יהוה אלה ים
על הארץ
ואדם אין
לעבד את
הארץ

ואד יעלה
מן הארץ
והשקה את
כל פני
הארץ וייצר
יהוה אלהים
את האדם

אד
דם

האדמה

ILLA TERRA VIRGO PLUVIS IRRIGATA

אם

figure 4

Our Stone proceeds first from the hand of God, or otherwise said, from י of יהוה.
Here is wisdom concerning the Operation: "For Jehovah Elohim had not caused it to rain upon the earth. And there was not a man to till the ground. But there went up a mist from the earth and watered the whole face of the earth. Then Jehovah Elohim formed the man." In the name of Adam is this concealed and revealed: For אם is the mother who is אדמה the red earth, virgin and unploughed, who produces a mist אד which is blood דם. From the seed of י there cometh Adam אדם the first man.

figure 5

And Adam was planted in the garden, eastward of Eden. And he was moulded from the clay like a statue, without Life: the first Man, from the earth, of dust. There he grew like a flower. Lo, the Holy Spirit breathed into his nostrils the breath of Life, and Man became a living Soul. Then he said, "My Soul magnifies the Lord!" For God had become Man.

Thus know that God becoming Man is INCREASE.
But Man becoming God is DECREASE

SOL PHILOSOPHORUM

LUNA PHILOSOPHORUM

ΧΡΥΣΑΝΘΕΜΟΝ

figure 6

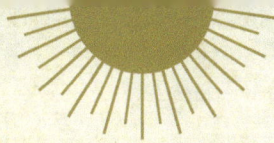

ow the flower that blooms in Eden is twofold. It is called by some the Sunflower.

By others it is known as the Moon Plant. But Wisdom informeth us that it is both of these at once; Sun and Moon, Male and Female, Adam and Eve. Thus, its true name is the Golden Flower.

figure 7

This, our Adam, we call the INFORMING MATERIAL or First Stone. Yet, the old must give way to the new. Thus it is written, "And the Earth brought forth the tree bearing fruit whose seed was in itself, after its kind."

And further, "Be patient therefore brethren, till the coming of the Lord. Lo, the husbandman awaits the precious fruit of the earth, being patient for it until it receives the early and latter rain."

Therefore Christ called himself BEN-ADAM, that is, SON OF MAN. So also, it has been written that the First Man Adam became a Living SOUL; the last Adam a quickening SPIRIT.

figure 8

ehold now Nature's sacrifice: the ripened fruit upon the vine. The twice-born Son of Man is slain, to pour his life into the earth: a rain of blood to quench her thirst - a worthy gift of little price, the secret stone of Magistry.

The First Stone is one with the Last Stone which the builders rejected for its uncomeliness. We call it Christ, the FUGITIVE, for it is hard to find. Because he is a fugitive, he is crucified among thieves. He is the Fruit of the Vine whose blood satisfied the hungry earth; whose blood fills the Moon till her countenance is Ruddy. Search for it in AKELDAMA, the Field of Blood when SATURN is visible.

SERPENS MECVRIALIS

ΝΕΚΡΟΣ

ΩΣΠΕΡ ΓΑΡ ΗΝ
ΙΩΝΑΣ ΕΝ ΤΗ
ΚΟΙΛΙΑ ΤΟΥ ΚΗΤΟΥΣ
ΤΡΕΙΣ ΗΜΕΡΑΣ
ΚΑΙ ΤΡΕΙΣ ΝΥΚΤΑΣ
ΟΥΤΩΣ ΕΣΤΑΙ Ο ΥΙΟΣ
ΤΟΥ ΑΝΘΡΩΠΟΥ ΕΝ
ΤΗ ΚΑΡΔΙΑ ΤΗΣ ΓΗΣ
ΤΡΕΙΣ ΗΜΕΡΑΣ
ΚΑΙ ΤΡΕΙΣ
ΝΥΚΤΟΣ

ΚΑΙ ΚΡΑΞΑΣ ΦΩΝΗ
ΜΕΓΑΛΗ ΑΦΗΚΕΝ ΤΟ
ΠΝΕΥΜΑ ΚΑΙ ΙΔΟΥ ΤΟ
ΚΑΤΑΠΕΤΑΣΜΑ ΤΟΥ
ΝΑΟΥ ΕΣΧΙΣΘΗ ΕΙΣ
ΔΥΟ ΑΠΟ ΑΝΩΘΕΝ
ΕΩΣ ΚΑΤΟ ΚΑΙ Η
ΓΗ ΕΣΕΙΣΘΗ ΚΑΙ ΑΙ
ΠΕΤΡΑΙ ΕΣΧΙΣΘΗΣΑΝ
ΚΑΙ ΤΑ ΜΝΗΜΕΙΑ
ΑΝΕΩΧΘΗΣΑΝ

ΑΔΗΣ
ΓΕΕΝΝΑ
ΤΑΡΤΑΡΟΣ

נחש

משיח

DESCENSVS

figure 9

Upon the sacred cross of death fair Hermes hangèd serpentine. With breath blown cold and pallid face, no more the fleeting savior god to race unseen through Heaven's course with rod erect and flashing eyes that guide the path of mortal flesh. He now descends into the grave whose mouth gapes wide in hungry haste to savor seed of God's own son, a journey deep into the womb where none but God hath eye to see. Here is the tomb wherein he lies, the hellish pit where night doth reign.

This is the second death and a great key to the quest for the Stone. For Christ goeth forth as the Mercurial Serpent to probe the depths of the Underworld. "For even as Jonah was in the belly of the fish for three days and three nights, so shall the Son of Man be in the heart of the earth three days and three nights." And having cried out with a loud voice he yielded up the Spirit. And behold, the veil of the Temple was rent in twain from top to bottom; and the earth was shaken and the rocks were rent, and the Tombs were opened. Now, the first day he is in HADES; the second, in GEHENNA. And the third, in TARTARUS, the deepest pit of Hell. Despair not. The darkest hour precedes the dawn.

עשה לך שרף ושים
אתו על־נס והיה
כל־הנשוך וראה
אתו וחי

שרף

Θεῖον

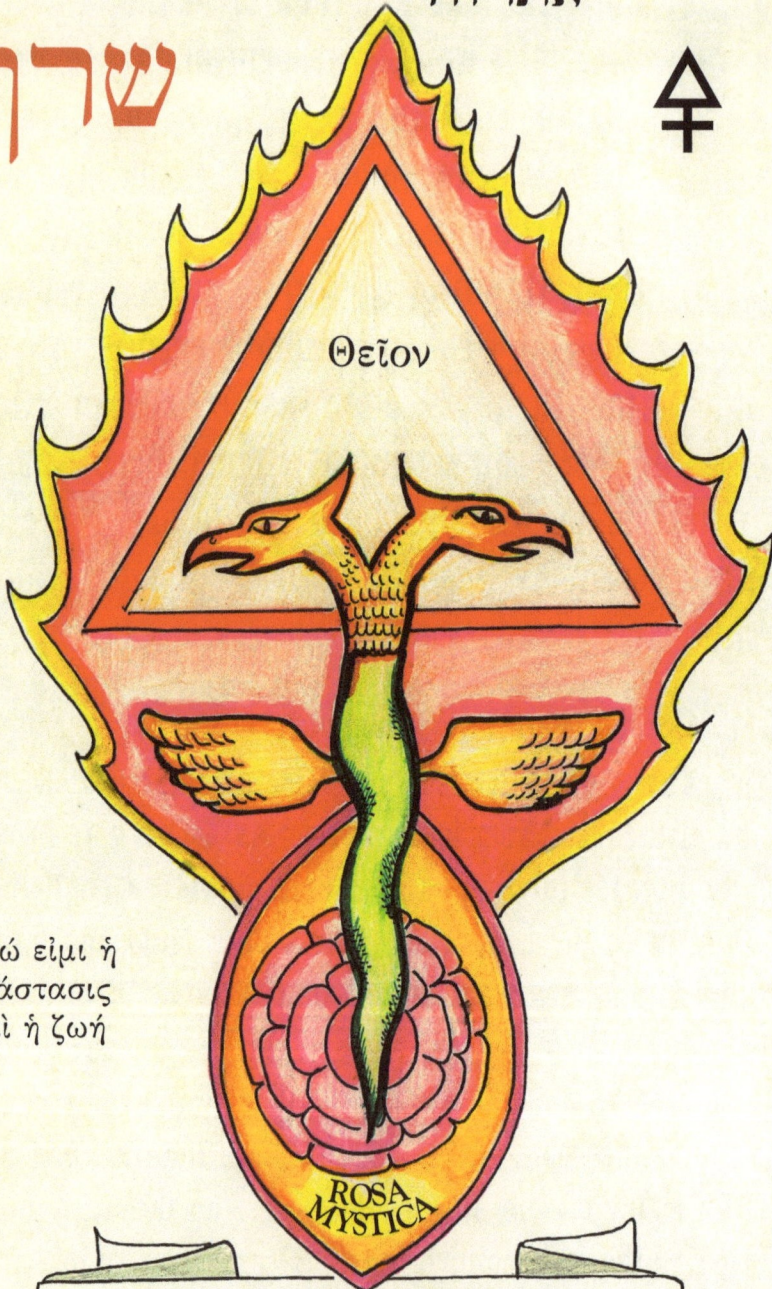

Ἐγώ εἰμι ἡ
ἀνάστασις
καὶ ἡ ζωή

ROSA
MYSTICA

QUI IUXTA ME EST, IUXTA
IGNEM EST, QUI LONGE EST A
ME, LONGE EST A REGNO

figure 10

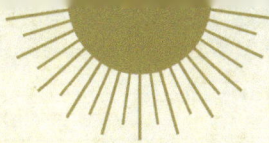

After three days in the Womb, Mercury is transformed into Sulphur, Θεῖον, which cometh from Θεῖος, "godhead". The Mercurial Serpent becomes the wingéd, twin-headed SERAPH, or Flaming Serpent, called by the Egyptians the Bennu Bird and by the Greeks, Phoenix. Therefore he said, "I am the Resurrection and the Life." And also, "He that is near to me, is near the fire. He that is far from me, is far from the Kingdom." Thus God commanded Moses, "Make thee a Fiery Serpent, and set it upon a pole and it shall come to pass that everyone that is bitten, when he looketh upon it, shall live."

ILLUMINATIO

VIS ANIMANS

καὶ οὐδεὶς ἀναβέβηκεν εἰς τὸν οὐρανὸν εἰ μὴ ὁ ἐκ τοῦ οὐρανοῦ καταβάς ὁ υἱὸς τοῦ ἀνθρώπου ὁ ὢν ἐν τῷ οὐρανῷ·

καὶ καθὼς Μωσῆς ὕψωσεν τὸν ὄφιν ἐν τῇ ἐρήμῳ οὕτως ὑψωθῆναι δεῖ τὸν υἱὸν τοῦ ἀνθρώπου· ἵνα πᾶς ὁ πιστεύων ἐν αὐτῷ μὴ ἀπόληται, ἀλλ᾽ ἔχῃ ζωὴν αἰώνιον.

ASCENSUS

ΩΣΠΕΡ ΓΑΡ ΕΝ ΤΩ ΑΔΑΜ ΠΑΝΤΕΣ ΑΠΟΘΝΗΣΚΟΥΣΙΝ
ΟΥΤΩΣ ΚΑΙ ΕΝ ΤΩ ΧΡΙΣΤΩ ΠΑΝΤΕΣ ΖΩΟΠΟΙΗΘΗΣΟΝΤΑΙ

figure 11

And no man hath ascended up to Heaven, but he that came down from Heaven even as the Son of Man which is in Heaven. And as Moses lifted up the Serpent in the wilderness, even so must the Son of Man be lifted up; that whosoever believeth in him should not perish but have Eternal Life. For in Adam all die, so also in Christ all shall be made alive.

Λίθον ὃν ἀπεδοκίμασαν οἱ οἰκοδομοῦντες, οὗτος ἐγενήθη εἰς κεφαλὴν γωνίας·

ϨΟΤΑΝ ΕΤΕΤΝϢⲀⲢ̄ ΠⲤΝΑⲨ ΟⲨⲀ ΑⲨⲰ Ε
ΤΕΤΝϢⲀⲢ̄ ΠⲤⲀ ΝϨΟⲨΝ Ν̄ΘΕ Μ̄ΠⲤⲀ ΝΒΟⲖ
ΑⲨⲰ ΠⲤⲀ̄ ΝΒΟⲖ Ν̄ΘΕ Μ̄ΠⲤⲀ ΝϨΟⲨΝ ΑⲨⲰ ΠⲤⲀ̄
ΤΠΕ Ν̄ΘΕ Μ̄ ⲤⲀ ⲘΠΙΤΝ̄ ΑⲨⲰ ϢΙΝⲀ ΕΤΕ
ΤΝⲀΕΙⲢΕ Μ̄ΦΟ ΟⲨⲦ ΜΝ̄ ΤⲤϨΙⲘΕ Μ̄ΠΙΟⲨⲀ
ΟⲨⲰⲦ ⲬΕΚⲀⲀⲤ ΝΕϤϨΟΟⲨⲦ Ⲣ̄ ϨΟΟⲨⲦ Ν̄ΤΕ
ΤⲤϨΙⲘΕ Ⲣ̄ ⲤϨΙⲘΕ ϨΟΤΑΝ ΕΤΕΤΝϢⲀϨΕΙⲢΕ
Ν̄ϨⲚ̄ΒⲀⲖ ΕΠⲘⲀ Ν̄ΟⲨΒⲀⲖ ΑⲨⲰ ΟⲨϬΙϪ̀
ΕΠⲘⲀ Ν̄ΝΟⲨϬΙϪ̀ ΑⲨⲰ ΟⲨΕⲢⲎⲦΕ ΕΠⲘⲀ
Ν̄ΟⲨΕⲢⲎⲦΕ ΟⲨϨΙΚⲰΝ ΕΠⲘⲀ Ν̄ΟⲨϨΙΚⲰ
ΤΟΤΕ ΤΕΤΝⲀΒⲰΚ ΕϨΟⲨΝ ΕΤⲘΝ̄ΤΕⲢΟ·

figure 12

Lo, the Stone which the builders rejected
has become the head of the corner. As
Didymos Judas Thomas revealed unto us
in his epistle,
When you make the two as one,
and when you make the inner as the outer
and the outer as the inner,
and the upper as the lower,
and when you make the male and the female into
a Single One,
so that the male will not be male and the female
will not be female,
when you make Eyes in the place of an eye,
and a Hand in the place of a hand,
and a Foot in the place of a foot,
an Image in the place of an image,
then you shall enter the Kingdom.

Amen

Ἄγγελος γὰρ κατὰ καιρὸν κατέβαινεν ἐν τῇ κολυμβήθρᾳ, καὶ ἐτάρασσεν τὸ ὕδωρ· ὁ οὖν πρῶτος ἐμβὰς μετὰ τὴν ταραχὴν τοῦ ὕδατος, ὑγιὴς ἐγίνετο, ᾧ δήποτε κατείχετο νοσήματι.

Ἐρημία

Πηγῆς τοῦ ὕδατος τῆς ζωῆς

ΜΟΝΟΚΕΡΩΣ ΕΣΤΙΝ ΟΥΤΟΣ ΖΩΟΝ ΑΥΤΟΝΟΜΟΝ

figure 13

FUNDAMENTUM ARTIS EST SOL ET EIUS UMBRA

SOL NIGER

figure 14

ORBIS STELLARUM

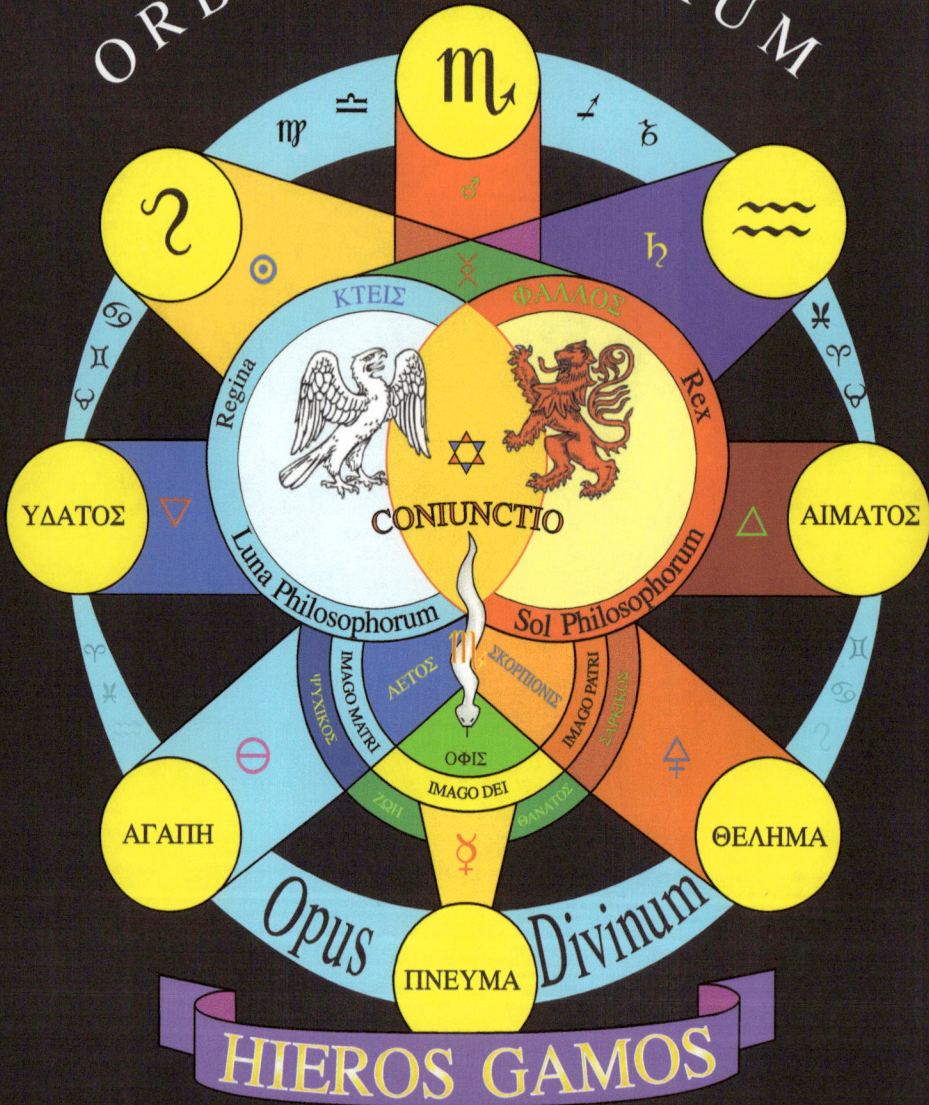

ΚΤΕΙΣ ΦΑΛΛΟΣ

Regina Rex

CONIUNCTIO

ΥΔΑΤΟΣ ΑΙΜΑΤΟΣ

Luna Philosophorum Sol Philosophorum

IMAGO MATRI IMAGO PATRI
ΨΥΧΙΚΟΣ ΑΕΤΟΣ ΣΚΟΡΠΙΟΝΙΣ ΣΑΡΚΙΚΟΣ
ΟΦΙΣ
ΖΩΗ IMAGO DEI ΘΑΝΑΤΟΣ

ΑΓΑΠΗ ΘΕΛΗΜΑ

Opus Divinum

ΠΝΕΥΜΑ

HIEROS GAMOS

Opus Alchymicum

Translations
&
Notes

Figure One

OPUS ALCHYMICUM
The Alchymical Work

SPIRITUS MERCURIALIS
The Spirit Mercury [The Guide]

ACETUM FONTIS
Corrosive Water [Vinegar of the Fountain]

AQUA VITAE
Water of Life [Fountain of the..]

Χριστός
Christ

Ἀετός
Eagle

Λέων
Lion

Πνεύματι ἁγίῳ
Holy Spirit

ἥλιος ἀνατολή
Rising Sun

Ἐν ἀρχῇ ἦν ὁ Λόγος, καὶ ὁ Λόγος ἦν πρὸς τὸν Θεόν, καὶ Θεὸς ἦν ὁ Λόγος.
In the beginning was the Word, and the Word was with God, and the Word was God.

John 1:1

Τοὔνεκ᾽ ἀπ᾽ αἰθερίου μεμερίσμεθα πνεύματος ἕλκειν.
Therefore it is our destiny to breath in the Spirit of the Aether.

Stobaeus' Anthologium 1.5.14

רוח אלהים
Ruach Elohim

Figure Two

IGNE NATURA RENOVATUR INTEGRA
The Whole of Nature is Renewed by Fire [By Fire Nature is Renewed Whole]

DONUM SPIRITUS SANCTI
Gift of the Holy Spirit [The Precious Gift]

PRIMA MATERIA
The First Matter [lowest form of ☿]

LAPIS NOSTER HIC EST IGNIS EX IGNE CREATUS ET IN IGNUM
VERTITUR, ET ANIMA EIUS IN IGNE MORATUR
This Our Stone is Fire, Created of Fire, and turns into Fire; its Soul dwells in Fire.

אש דם מים
Fire, Blood, Water [All concealed in the name of ADAM]

פרי עץ
Fruit of the Tree

גולגלתא
Golgotha

Figure Three

DIVIDE LAPIDEM TUUM IN QUATUOR ELEMENTA
ET CONIUNGE IN UNUM ET TOTUM HABEBIS MAGISTERIUM
Divide your Stone into four elements, and unite it into One, and you will have the whole Magistery.

ΑΔΑΜ
Adam

Καρδία
Heart

στρογγύλος καὶ τετράγωνος
Round and Square

פישון
Pison

גיחון
Gihon

חדקל
Hiddakel

פרת
Phrath

עדן
Eden

Figure Four

ILLA TERRA VIRGO PLUVIS IRRIGATA
That Virgin Earth Watered by Rain

יוד יהוה
The Hand of God

אד
Vapor

דם
Blood

האדמה
The Earth

אם
Mother

לא המטיר יהוה אלהים על הארץ ואדם אין לעבד את הארץ
ואד יעלה מן הארץ והשקה את כל פני הארץ   וייצר
יהוה אלהים את האדם

For the LORD God had not caused it to rain upon the earth, and there was not a man
to till the earth. [note: the modified word is 'ground' האדמה to 'earth' הארץ]
But there went up a mist from the earth, and watered the whole face of the ground.
And the LORD God formed man of the dust *of* the ground.

Genesis 2:5-7

Figure Five

Μεγαλύνει ἡ ψυχή μου τὸν κύριον
My soul magnifies the Lord

Source: And Mary said, My soul doth magnify the Lord.

Luke 1:46

ὁ πρῶτος ἄνθρωπος ἐκ γῆς χοϊκός
The first man from the earth, made of dust;

Source: The first man was of the earth, made of dust; the second Man is the Lord from heaven.
[It should be noted here that the Greek has a somewhat different translation of the second half of the verse, which is as follows: 'the second Man from heaven.']

1 Corinthians 15:47

נפשת חיים
Soul of Life

Author's note: The Holy Spirit, Ruach Elohim, descending breathing into Man the Breath of LIFE.

האדמה
The Earth

ויהי האדם לנפש חיה
Man became a living soul

Source: And the Lord God formed man of the dust of the ground, and breathed into his nostrils the breath of life; and man became a living soul.

Genesis 2:7

Author's note: Adam assumes the position of Osiris as corn god growing from the ground ADAMAH. Golden rays emanate from the clay man suggesting a flower. About the rays in Greek 'My soul magnifies the Lord' – for God ever desires to be man. Beneath the Rays, on the bottom in Greek 'the first man from the Earth of dust.' On the lower banner in Hebrew 'and man became a living soul.'

Figure Six

SOL PHILOSOPHORUM
The Philosophical sun [The Sun of the Philosophers]

LUNA PHILOSOPHORUM
The Philosophical Moon [The Moon of the Philosophers]

ΧΡΥΣΑΝΘΕΜΟΝ
Chrysanthemum

Translation below from the study which is found in the first and second edition.

ὁ πρῶτος ἄνθρωπος ὅμοιος λέοντι
The first man is like a lion

ἤ γυνὴ ὁμοία ἀετῷ πετομένῳ
The woman was like a flying eagle

Source: And the first beast was like a lion, and the second beast like a calf, and the third beast had a face as a man, and the fourth beast was like a flying eagle.

Revelation 4:7

Figure Seven

SOLIFICATIO
Showing Forth of the Sun

HOMO MAXIMUS
The Highest Man

FILIUS PHILOSOPHORUM
The Philosophical Child [Child of the Philosophies]

ARBOR PHILOSOPHICA
The Philosophical Tree

MATERIA INFORMIS (or MATERIA CONFUSA = Χάος)
Shapeless Matter [which contains divine seeds ever since creation]

ΠΝΕΫΜΑ
Spirit

ΨΫΧΗ
Psyche

τοῦ γενήματος τῆς ἀμπέλου
The Fruit of the Vine

Source: But I say unto you, I will not drink henceforth of this fruit of the vine, until
that day when I drink it new with you in my Father's kingdom.

Matthew 26:29

οὕτως καὶ γέγραπται Ἐγένετο ὁ πρῶτος ἄνθρωπος Ἀδὰμ εἰς ψυχὴν ζῶσαν· ὁ
ἔσχατος Ἀδὰμ εἰς πνεῦμα ζωοποιοῦν.
So also it has been written, the first man Adam was made a living soul; the last Adam
was made a quickening spirit.

1 Corinthians 15:45

Μακροθυμήσατε οὖν ἀδελφοί ἕως τῆς παρουσίας τοῦ κυρίου ἰδού, ὁ γεωργὸς ἐκδέχεται τὸν τίμιον καρπὸν τῆς γῆς μακροθυμῶν ἐπ᾽ αὐτῷ ἕως ἂν λάβῃ ὑετὸν πρώϊμον καὶ ὄψιμον.

Be patient therefore, brethren, unto the coming of the Lord. Behold, the husbandman waiteth for the precious fruit of the earth, and hath long patience for it, until he receive the early and latter rain. [Be ye also patient; stablish your hearts: for the coming of the Lord draweth nigh.]

James 5:7

אדם
Adam

ותוצא הארץ העץ עשה פרי אשר זרע בו למינהו
And the earth brought forth the tree bearing fruit whose seed was in itself, after its kind.

Genesis 1:12

And the earth brought forth grass, and herb yielding seed after his kind, and the tree yielding fruit, whose seed was in itself, according to its kind: [note: *A portion of the verse in Hebrew is in the manuscript, see the accompanying text*]

Figure Eight

IMAGO LAPIDIS
Image of the Stone [of Christ as an Image of the stone]

FUGITIVUS
The Fugitive

Ἀκελδαμά Χωρίον Αἵματος
Akeldama Field of Blood

Source: And it was known unto all the dwellers at Jerusalem; insomuch as that field is called in their proper tongue, Aceldama, that is to say, The field of blood.

Acts 1:19

Λίθον ὃν ἀπεδοκίμασαν οἱ οἰκοδομοῦντες
The stone which the builders rejected

Source: And have ye not read this scripture; The stone which the builders rejected is become the head of the corner.

Mark 12:10

αὐτομάτη ἡ γῆ καρποφορεῖ, ὅταν δὲ παραδοῖ ὁ καρπός, εὐθὺς ἀποστέλλει τὸ δρέπανον, ὅτι παρέστηκεν ὁ θερισμός.
For the earth bringeth forth fruit of herself; immediately he sends forth the sickle, because the harvest is come.

Source: For the earth bringeth forth fruit of herself; first the blade, then the ear, after that the full corn in the ear. But when the fruit is brought forth, immediately he putteth in the sickle, because the harvest is come.

Mark 4:28 & 29

תו
Cross

Figure Nine

SERPENS MECVRIALIS [SERPENS MERCVRIALIS]
Mercurial Serpent

DESCENSVS
Descent

ΝΕΚΡΟΣ
Dead

ΑΔΗΣ
Hades

ΓΕΕΝΝΑ
Gehenna

ΤΑΡΤΑΡΟΣ
Tartarus

נחש
Serpent

משיח
Messiah

ΩΣΠΕΡ ΓΑΡ ΗΝ ΙΩΝΑΣ ΕΝ ΤΗ ΚΟΙΛΙΑ ΤΟΥ ΚΗΤΟΥΣ ΤΡΕΙΣ ΗΜΕΡΑΣ
ΚΑΙ ΤΡΕΙΣ ΝΥΚΤΑΣ ΟΥΤΩΣ ΕΣΤΑΙ Ο ΥΙΟΣ ΤΟΥ ΑΝΘΡΩΠΟΥ ΕΝ ΤΗ
ΚΑΡΔΙΑ ΤΗΣ ΓΗΣ ΤΡΕΙΣ ΗΜΕΡΑΣ ΚΑΙ ΤΡΕΙΣ ΝΥΚΤΟΣ

ὥσπερ γὰρ ἦν Ἰωνᾶς ἐν τῇ κοιλίᾳ τοῦ κήτους τρεῖς ἡμέρας καὶ τρεῖς νύκτας,
οὕτως ἔσται ὁ υἱὸς τοῦ ἀνθρώπου ἐν τῇ καρδίᾳ τῆς γῆς τρεῖς ἡμέρας καὶ τρεῖς
νύκτας.
For as Jonas was three days and three nights in the whale's belly; so shall the Son of
man be three days and three nights in the heart of the earth.

Mathew 12:40

51

ΚΑΙ ΚΡΑΞΑΣ ΦΩΝΗ ΜΕΓΑΛΗ ΑΦΗΚΕΝ ΤΟ ΠΗΕΥΜΑ ΚΑΙ ΙΔΟΥ ΤΟ
ΚΑΤΑΠΕΤΑΣΜΑ ΤΟΥ ΝΑΟΥ ΕΣΧΙΣΘΝ ΕΙΣ ΔΥΟ ΑΠΟ ΑΝΩΘΕΝ ΕΩΣ ΚΑΤΟ
ΚΑΙ Η ΓΗ ΕΣΕΙΣΘΗ ΚΑΙ ΑΙ ΠΕΤΡΑΙ ΕΣΧΙΣΘΗΣΑΝ ΚΑΙ ΤΑ ΜΝΗΜΕΙΑ
ΑΝΕΩΧΘΗΣΑΝ

[Καὶ] κράξας φωνῇ μεγάλη ἀφῆκεν τὸ πνεῦμα. Καὶ ἰδοὺ τὸ καταπέτασμα τοῦ
ναοῦ ἐσχίσθη ἀπ' ἄνωθεν ἔως κάτω εἰς δύο, καὶ ἡ γῆ ἐσείσθη, καὶ αἱ πέτραι
ἐσχίσθησαν, καὶ τὰ μνημεῖα ἀνεῴχθησαν
[And] having cried with a loud voice, yielded up the Spirit. And, behold, the veil of the
temple was rent in twain from the top to the bottom; and the earth did quake, and the
rocks rent; And the graves were opened.

Matthew 27:50-52

Figure Ten

QUI IUXTA ME EST, IUXTA IGNEM EST, QUI LONGE EST A ME, LONGE
EST A REGNO
He that is near to Me is near the Fire, He that is far from Me is far from the Kingdom.

Source: Jesus said, He who is near me is near the fire, and he who is far from me is far
from the kingdom.

Gospel of Thomas 82

ROSA MYSTICA
Mystic Rose

Θεῖον
Sulphur [derived from Θεῖος 'Godhead']

Ἐγώ εἰμι ἡ ἀνάστασις καὶ ἡ ζωή
I am the resurrection, and the life.

Source: Jesus said unto her, I am the resurrection, and the life: he that believeth in me,
though he were dead, yet shall he live.

John 11:25

עשה לך שרף ושים אתו על־נס והיה כל־הנשוך וראה אתו וחי

Make thee a fiery serpent, and set it upon a pole: and it shall come to pass, that every one that is bitten, when he looketh upon it, shall live.

Numbers 21:8

ποίησον σεαυτῷ ὄφιν καὶ θὲς αὐτὸν ἐπὶ σημείου, καὶ ἔσται ἐὰν δάκη ὄφις ἄνθρωπον, πᾶς ὁ δεδηγμένος ἰδὼν αὐτὸν ζήσεται.

Septuagint

שרף
Seraph [Flaming Serpent]

Figure Eleven

ILLUMINATIO
Enlightened [corresponds to SOLIFICATIO]

VIS ANIMANS
Life Force

ASCENSUS
Ascent

καὶ οὐδεὶς ἀναβέβηκεν εἰς τὸν οὐρανὸν εἰ μὴ ὁ ἐκ τοῦ οὐρανοῦ καταβάς ὁ υἱὸς τοῦ ἀνθρώπου ὁ ὢν ἐν τῷ οὐρανῷ· καὶ καθὼς Μωσῆς ὕψωσεν τὸν ὄφιν ἐν τῇ ἐρήμῳ οὕτως ὑψωθῆναι δεῖ τὸν υἱὸν τοῦ ἀνθρώπου· ἵνα πᾶς ὁ πιστεύων ἐν αὐτῷ μὴ ἀπόληται, ἀλλ᾽ ἔχῃ ζωὴν αἰώνιον.

And no man hath ascended up to heaven, but he that came down from heaven, even the Son of man which is in heaven. And as Moses lifted up the serpent in the wilderness, even so must the son of man be lifted up: That whosoever believeth in him should not perish, but have eternal life.

John 3:13-15

ΩΣΠΕΡ ΓΑΡ ΕΝ ΤΩ ΑΔΑΜ ΠΑΝΤΕΣ ΑΠΟΘΝΗΣΚΟΥΣΙΝ
ΟΥΤΩΣ ΚΑΙ ΕΝ ΤΩ ΧΡΙΣΤΩ ΠΑΝΤΕΣ ΖΩΟΠΟΙΗΘΗΣΟΝΤΑΙ
For as in Adam all die, even so in Christ shall all be made alive.

1 Corinthians 15:22

Figure Twelve

Λίθον ὃν ἀπεδοκίμασαν οἱ οἰκοδομοῦντες, οὗτος ἐγενήθη εἰς κεφαλὴν γωνίας·
The stone which the builders rejected is become the head of the corner.

Source: And have ye not read this scripture; The stone which the builders rejected is become the head of the corner.

Mark 12:10

ϩΟΤΑΝ ΕΤΕΤΝ͞ϢΑ͞Ρ ΠⲤΝΑ͞ϒ ΟϒΑ Αϒω Ε
ΤΕΤΝ͞ϢΑ͞Ρ ΠⲤΑ ΝϩΟϒΝ Ν͞ΘΕ Μ͞ΠⲤΑ ΝΒΟⲖ
Αϒω ΠⲤΑ͞ ΝΒΟⲖ Ν͞ΘΕ Μ͞ΠⲤΑ ΝϩΟϒΝ Αϒω ΠⲤΑ͞
ΤΠΕ Ν͞ΘΕ Μ͞ⲤΑ Μ͞ΠΙΤΝ͞ Αϒω ϢΙΝΑ ΕΤΕ
ΤΝΑΕΙΡΕ Μ͞ΦΟ ΟϒΤ Μ͞Ν ΤⲤϩΙΜΕ Μ͞ΠΙΟϒΑ
ΟϒωΤ ΧΕΚΑΑⲤ ΝΕΦΟΟϒΤ Ρ͞ ϩΟΟϒΤ Ν͞ΤΕ
ΤⲤϩΙΜΕ Ρ͞ ⲤϩΙΜΕ ϩΟΤΑΝ ΕΤΕΤΝ͞ϢΑΕΙΡΕ
Ν͞ϩΝΒΑⲖ ΕΠΜΑ Ν͞ΟϒΒΑⲖ Αϒω ΟϒϬΙΧ
ΕΠΜΑ Ν͞ΝΟϒϬΙΧ Αϒω ΟϒΕΡΗΤΕ ΕΠΜΑ
Ν͞ΟϒΕΡΗΤΕ ΟϒϩΙΚωΝ ΕΠΜΑ Ν͞ΟϒϩΙΚω͞
ΤΟΤΕ ΤΕΤΝΑΒωΚ ΕϩΟϒΝ ΕΤΜΝ͞ΤΕΡΟ

When you make the two as one,
and when you make the inner as the outer and the outer as the inner,
and the upper as the lower,
and when you make the male and the female into a Single One,
so that the male will not be male and the female will not be female,
when you make Eyes in the place of an eye,
and a Hand in the place of a hand,
and a Foot in the place of a foot,
an Image in the place of an image,
then you shall enter the Kingdom.

The Gospel of Thomas Log. 22

Figure Thirteen

Ἐρημία
Wilderness

Πηγῆς τοῦ ὕδατος τῆς ζωῆς
Source of the Water of Life

ΜΟΝΟΚΕΡΩΣ ΕΣΤΙΝ ΟΥΤΟΣ ΖΩΟΝ ΑΥΤΟΝΟΜΟΝ
The Unicorn is a self-ruled living thing

Patrologiae Cursus Completus, Vol. 120 p. 112. (Greek 1439)

Ἄγγελος γὰρ κατὰ καιρὸν κατέβαινεν ἐν τῇ κολυμβήθρᾳ, καὶ ἐτάρασσεν τὸ
ὕδωρ· ὁ οὖν πρῶτος ἐμβὰς μετὰ τὴν ταραχὴν τοῦ ὕδατος, ὑγιὴς ἐγίνετο, ᾧ
δήποτε κατείχετο νοσήματι.
**For an angel went down at a certain season into the pool, and troubled the water:
whosoever then first after the troubling of the water stepped in was made whole of
whatsoever disease he had.**

John 5:4

Figure Fourteen

FUNDAMENTUM ARTIS EST SOL ET EIUS UMBRA
The basis of the Art is the Sun and its Shadow

Rosarium Philosophorum, in *Artis Auriferae*, Vol. 2 (1593) p. 233

SOL NIGER
The Black Sun

Notes on the Stone of the Philosophers

QUEMADMODUM IN SOLE AMBULANTIS CORPUS CONTINUO SEQUITUR
UMBRA SIC HERMAPHRODITUS NOSTER ADAMICUS, QUAMIS IN FORMA
MASCULI APPAREAT SEMPER TAMEN IN CORPORE OCCULTATAM EVAM
SIVE FOEMINAM SUAM SECUM CIRCUMFERT
As the shadow continually follows the body of one who walks in the sun, so our
hermaphroditic Adam, though he appears in the form of a male, nevertheless always
carries about with him Eve, or his wife, hidden in his body.

Mangetus, Bibliotheca Chemica Curiosa, Vol. 1, p. 417 (Geneva 1702)

UNUM ET EST DUO, ET DUO ET SUNT TRIA, ET TRIA ET SUNT
QUATUOR, ET QUATUOR ET SUNT TRIA, ET TRIA ET SUNT DUO, ET
DUO ET SUNT UNUM
One, and it is two; and two, and it is three; and three, and it is four; and four, and it is
three; and three, and it is two; and two, and it is one. [cf. יהוה as diagram of creation]

Allegoriae Sapientum, in Theatrum Chemicum, Vol. 5 (1622) p. 86

NEC INTRAT IN EUM, QUOD NON SIT ORTUM EX EO, QUONIAM SI
ALIQUID EXTRANEI SIBI APPONATUR, STATIM CORRUMPITUR.
Nothing enters into it [the Stone=LAPIDEM] that did not come from it; since, if
anything extraneous were to be added to it, it would at once be corrupted.

Rosarium Philosophorum, in Artis Auriferae, Vol. 2 (1593) p. 213

IN AURO SUNT QUATUOR ELEMENTA IN AEQUALI PROPORTIONE
APTATA.
In the gold, the four elements are contained in equal proportion.

Rosarium Philosophorum, in Artis Auriferae, Vol. 2 (1593) p. 208

LAPIS NOSTER EST EX QUATUOR ELEMENTIS.
Our Stone is from the four elements.

Rosarium Philosophorum, in Artis Auriferae, Vol. 2 (1593) page 207

Notes on Alchemy

Anima Mundi – Soul of the World
Aqua Permanes – The Permanent Water
Circulatio – Circulation (The Wheel)
Circumambulation – Going in a Circle (necessary to transform the life mass)
Exilis – Uncomely (The Stone that the builders rejected)
Familiaris – A Familiar (☿ as familiar since he is close to the Sun)
Fons Signatus – A Fountain Sealed (The VIRGIN)
Lapis Invisibilitatis – Stone of Invisibility
Lapis Philosophorum – The Stone of the Philosophers (highest form of ☿)
Succus Lunariae – Sap of the Moon Plant
Tinictura Rubea – The Red Tincture
Vas Bene Clausum – Well Sealed Vessel (Magick Circle)

FIN

The Greek is sourced from Westcott and Hort 1881 &
Stephanus Textus Receptus 1550 or as noted.
The English Bible text is from KJV.
Latin is taken from notes by the author or as noted.
Hebrew is standard or from notes by the author.
Coptic is from The Gospel of Thomas.

Afterword

"Here the dew falleth from heaven,
And washeth the black body in the sepulchre"
Rosarium Philosophorum, 1550.

In 2013 when the *Opus Alchymicum* prints were first shown at The Langue Verte exhibition in Perth, I was asked to write the Gallery press release. I penned:

> The Opus Alchymicum series records a transformative process of archetypal encounters with alchemical motifs. Experienced by the Artist through the late 1970s and early 1980s at a time of emotional and spiritual crisis, the transpersonal Self constellated in the psyche of the Artist to restore equilibrium and wholeness. From the depths of the Unconscious, alchemical images arose of the Great Return to the Supernal Eden, of transfiguration and redemption, in that great *coniunctio* – the hieros gamos – of the filius philosophorum.

J. Daniel Gunther's response was "You have it exactly right. EXACTLY RIGHT. I know I didn't tell you all of that, you surely just channeled it. Amazing really."[1]

But what was it that Gunther thought was 'exactly right'? I *think* it was that the *Opus Alchymicum* is a work of healing.

1 Gunther, J. Daniel (2013, pers. comm., 19 November).

Traditionally, the goal of the opus alchymicum ('the work of alchemy') was the *lapis philosophorum* or Stone of the Philosophers, the Universal Medicine described in the *Sophic Hydrolith* as the 'cure for all unsound and imperfect metals.' According to Zosimos of Panopolis, this transmutation of the unsound and imperfect could only be achieved by 'plunging into meditation.' Morienus taught that the alchemist must 'descend/ Into himself the matter for to find/of this our Stone.' Similar instructions are found throughout the literature. The *Opus Alchymicum* records a modern day descent, a task also referred to as the *opus contra naturam* ('the work against nature') – the turning back or great return to a divine source against the outward pull of nature, or the *opus circulatorium* ('the circular work of the elements') – the reiterative process of dissolution to the *prima materia* to then coagulate into the Stone. The *circulatio* inherent to this *solve et coagula* process suggests that access to the *Opus Alchymicum* may not be in the individual images *pars pro toto* but in the transitus between them, guided by the *dereistic* instruction of Eugnostos the blessed. Eugnostos lights the Way to the *lumen naturalis*, the inner light of the *Imago* (the series of images treated as a whole or mandala).

Whilst the *Opus Alchymicum* records an individual's descent, it is important to con-sider that the Imago encountered is not a personal cosmology. Nor is the Epistle of Eugnostos an ideolect unique to Gunther 'his beloved son.' Eugnostos is a figure of Self, transpersonal and collective to us all, with such threshold figures often guiding encounters with the Unconscious. His relationship to Gunther is similar to Philemon's with Carl Jung – the voice from within that was not himself. Likewise the images are symbols, universal rather than personal, illustrating the orientation to Self (the method and process of healing) as the psyche traverses the mandala wheel of the God-image.

In the encounter with the Unconscious, Jung was quite critical of the likes of Picasso and Joyce, feeling that they reveled in their descents into the Underworld as a type of artistic self indulgence. He saw them as remaining in the sensorium of the fantasy and not returning to the world, to hard reality, to the burden of western history, the Christian psyche. By refusing to return, they failed to partake of the Stone, the elixir, the tincture – that which is endowed with the Powers of the Above. There is no redemption. Jung followed Virgil, "Easy is the descent to Avernus ... but to recall your steps and pass out to the upper air, this is the task, this is the toil"[2] – to return to the world and to integrate, understand and ultimately develop the *Imago Dei*. There is something akin to this going on with the *Opus Alchymicum*, which up until now Gunther has kept private to himself and only a handful of students. In one sense its viewing beyond that small circle hasn't really mattered. What mattered was what Gunther did when he 'recalled his steps and passed out to the upper air.' The silent counsel of Eugnostos was to teach the lessons learned – for Gunther to make conscious the encounter with the Unconscious within the conceptual framework of the A∴A∴.The psychological response to such a task is that the *Opus Alchymicum* would, sooner or later, *force* itself into publication. The concepts stemming from its lmago have got out and the Unconscious responds by placing upon them its demands for wholeness and perspective.

In this sense it is telling that the *Opus Alchymicum* finds publication thirty five years after its reception. That's the psychological response mentioned above, a response with broad similarities to the circumstances behind Jung's *Red Book* and Goethe's (second part of) *Faust* – in both cases *magna opera* posthumously published. Jung wrote of *The Red Book* "My entire life consisted in elaborating what had burst forth from the unconscious and flooded me like an enigmatic stream that threatened to break me ... .

2 Virgil, Aeneid, VI, 126-29.

Everything later was merely the outer classification, the scientific elaboration, and the integration into life. But the numinous beginning, which contained everything, was then."[3]

Whilst the *Opus Alchymicum* might not be of the same magnitude (only Gunther could answer that), it certainly contains *something*, and it was a numinous beginning that would shape much of his later life and work – the outer classification and scientific elaboration of the Mysteries of the A∴A∴.. It is highly unlikely Gunther recognised that in 1979. I suspect Eugnostos did.

For the student with sensibility, the *Opus Alchymicum* reformulates how Gunther's later works can be comprehended. Here we glimpse the *artistic* elaboration of the System, its psychic experience, its lyric, its numinosity and continuity of the tradition. We get a better understanding of Gunther's recourse to alchemy and psychology in his books and lectures. We see it in practice so to speak. You could say that it is Eugnostos who has called for the publication of the *Opus Alchymicum* today. In doing so the *Opus* gets reformulated again, its archetypes alive and inviting a new encounter. *Opus circulatorium.* The 'beloved son' is now anyone who listens to Eugnostos; anyone who pursues *their* own opus; anyone who encounters the Christ Imago, Mercurius. Any ego that is 'blessed' or orients to Self.

The Opus Alchymicum commenced after Gunther broke from his teacher in the A∴A∴, the late Marcello Ramos Motta. It was a departure that left the student emotionally and spiritually shattered. Just prior to leaving Motta, Gunther had translated the passage from Stobaeus that opens the Epistle. Then shortly after Motta, he had what he described to me as a 'moving dream' of the alchemical sacred

---

3 Jung, Carl Gustav. *The Red Book: Liber Novus.* ed. Sonu Shamdasani. New York & London: W.W. Norton & Co (2009). Back cover.

marriage, the *Hieros Gamos*. The characters from that dream became figure one (Opus Alchymicum). The following night he dreamt of the crucified sun (I.N.R.I.) and so on and so forth. It was after staring at I.N.R.I. that Gunther said he could feel himself beginning to heal – he recognised that the image had a healing power for his fractured psyche. This acceptance was ultimately the catalyst for the rest of the *Opus*.

Gunther took to keeping small pieces of drawing paper, a black felt pen and coloured pencils by his bedside. After the dreams he would do the rough sketches.[4] Usually, he would then think about the image all day and that night do the larger drawing. A capable artist, Gunther intended to carefully and skilfully draw the larger images. However, in the white heat of the ongoing psychic process, he often rushed and the results at times can be hurried and crude.[5] This suggests he was in the grip of the archetypes.

The Biblical verses and other words in Greek, Hebrew or Coptic were either jotted down with the initial sketch, or at other times Gunther knew what was intended but had to look them up. Their translation or transliteration and gnostic speculation are given in the Epistle.

Often in the dreams ideas were conveyed symbolically by words and flashes, rather than the firm images that ended up on paper. Some images were not depicted as they were dreamt. For example, the Golden Flower (figure six) was a dream of Adam and Eve as a hermaphrodite, however the drawn image captured the essence of the dream's mystery. Sol Niger (figure fourteen) was dreamt with the Dark One standing in front of Gunther, but was sketched with a secondary figure in the background and later drawn solitary. These aesthetic changes were

---

4 For the surviving sketches, see pp. 31-34 (The sketches are found in the first and second edition-Editor)

5 Note for example the misspelt 'Mecurialis' in Serpens Mercurialis (figure 9).

made to enliven the archetypal motif rather than just record the dream's personal detail. Some of the drawings were executed later than the following night. Monokeros (figure thirteen), the second last in the series, was the final image drawn.

This is significant as Monokeros ('The Unicorn') was drawn *exactly* as it was dreamt. Gunther recalled:

> I was in a clearing in the midst of a forest, where there was a Fountain surmounted by a single fish. A Unicorn came out of the forest, and began to drink from the fountain. I was overcome with such a sense of peace. Then I awoke.[6]

In Jung's reading of alchemy and certainly within the *Opus Alchymicum*, the Unicorn is a Christ symbol and represents the Christ Imago or *Logos* that appears in different forms throughout the opus. In Monokeros it is retreating back into the Unconscious (represented by its complete animal form). Further, if you look at Monokeros, the Greek word above the forest, *erimiá*, means 'wilderness' i.e. Gunther was in a *Temenos*: The Unicorn drank from the fountain of life, and then retreated into the forest. I think at that moment, I had come to terms with my Christian childhood.[7]

That coming to terms with a Christian childhood was intrinsic to the healing process over Motta is striking. Whilst no doubt a personal and private matter, perhaps on another level it alludes to the ego-Self axis (or Christ as Self relating to the subordinate ego) and what happens when relationships expressive of that dichotomy lose their equilibrium and bring on Unconscious response. The Unicorn reminds us that ultimately we must fix the volatile by our own efforts through the formula '*Christus de Christo, Mercurius de Mercurio.*' In the years after the

6 Gunther, J. Daniel (2014, pers. Comm., 6 march)

7 Gunther, J. Daniel (2014, pers. Comm., 6 march)

Opus Alchymicum, Gunther would teach the same in his formulation of the A∴A∴ doctrine of the Star of the Messiah.[8]

The Opus Alchymicum concludes with Sol Niger (figure fourteen). In the literature, Sol Niger ('black sun') represents death and putrefaction or the union of Sulphur and Argent Vive (Mercury) during the *Nigredo*, the *initial* stage of the alchemical opus. Why does the Dark One now appear here at the end? We are faced with a *paradoxia*. On one level we end where we begun, the mandala wheel having gone full circle. On another, remembering the impetus behind the first image, the Dark One indicates that upon his return, Gunther would have to teach the Hieros Gamos to his students undertaking the Nigredo phase of the Great Work, for their resurrection in the sealing of the *Albedo* in Tiphareth.[9] In this sense Sol Niger undergoes a transformation – the archetypes evolve – and the Dark One is now the Holy Guardian Angel (the Angel of Death) and indicative of the formula Gunther would spend the rest of his life expounding: N.O.X. ('night', 'darkness').

It is fitting the *Opus Alchymicum* concludes with this figure, the Dark One concealing one of the primary instructions of the Holy Guardian Angel. Jung always treated images as ciphers and symbols, expressions of Self to be used in a quest for understanding. In the aftermath of the publication of *The Red Book* some of Jung's school have turned away from the language of analytical psychology and placed their focus on the image alone, dismantling the conceptual matrix and its scientific elaboration. The Dark One silently cautions against such a treatment of the *Opus Alchymicum*:

8 See Gunther, J. Daniel. Initiation in the Aeon of the Child: the Inward Journey. Lake Worth, FL: Ibis Books (2009) and The Angel & The Abyss. Lake Worth, FL: Ibis books (2014).

9 See The Angel & The Abyss, ibid. The frontispiece illustration of the Hieros Gamos may be treated as the culmination of the Opus Alchymicum. Its instruction is expounded throughout the book.

"Be not contented with the image. I who am the Image of an Image say this. Debate not of the image, saying Beyond! Beyond! One mounteth unto the Crown by the moon and by the Sun, and by the arrow, and by the Foundation, and by the dark home of the stars from the black earth. Not otherwise may you reach unto the Smooth Point." *Liber LXV*: I: 7-10.

Whilst 'Eugnostos the blessed' is the name of an Epistle in the Nag Hammadi Library (Codices III, V), Gunther was only made aware of this in 2014. He had however read the Nag Hammadi texts prior to the opus, so I think we can safely assume the name emerged from his personal unconscious. In the *Opus Alchymicum*, Eugnostos is treated as a proper name and is taken to mean 'the one who can know.'[10] The Epistle was written as a private meditation (some time after the cycle of dreams and images) and spontaneously took on a Gnostic form. This type of meditation was central to alchemical opera and in modern times can be likened to some of the techniques of the Jungian school's *active imagination*.

Whilst interpreting the detail of the *Opus Alchymicum* is in this place rightly left to each individual, some parting significance can be drawn from Eugnostos' dedication of the Epistle 'to his beloved son.' It introduces the notion of generation, indicating that the 'work of alchemy' is ultimately a descent into human ancestry, the ancestors, the collective, or in other words – the dead. The Epistle is their utterance in Gnostic and Qabalistic form. It's an averse position to that of Freud's *Tagesrest*, the notion that the unresolved residue from the day feeds

---

10 Eugnostos is a Greek adjective composed of eu, 'good' or 'well' and gnostos, 'known'. Eugnostos can mean 'well known,' 'familiar' (Plato Lysias, frag. 17.3) or 'easy to understand' (Plato Sophist 218e). It's opposite is agnostos, 'unknown,' a term used to indicate the supreme God (Epicurus On the Nature of Things 28.5). Its active meaning is 'the one who can know' or 'the one capable of knowing' (Philo of Alexandria On the Creation of the World 154) and it may be a synonym of the term gnostes ('the one who knows' Acts 26:3). See www.earlychristianwritings.com/eugnostos.html

the dreams of the night. Jung proposed that we are the result of these figures and images, not the other way around. Gunther embarks on a very similar approach, allowing these figures to show themselves and act upon him. To heal him. Death is the Gate to Life. Life is the Gate to Death. The *Opus Alchymicum* beckons us to return to the Supernal Eden, to switch our focus from a world which calls death life, to a world where True Life is death to the world.

This is the Great Work.

> "Not one item of the Christian law is abrogated, but instead we are adding a new one: accepting the lament of the dead."

> Jung, *The Red Book*.

Stephen J. King

The author at the time of writing Opus Alchymicum

About the Author

J. Daniel Gunther is considered one of the foremost scholar-practitioners of Thelema. He has authored several books that focus on the theology of Thelema while drawing on his extensive knowledge of Egyptology, Jungian Psychology, Qabalah, Alchemy, Gnosticism and Philosophy. He is also the artist and writer of original work on mystical Alchemy. Gunther's overview on the history of academic research in Egyptian religion and philology is published in the 20th Anniversary Edition of the *Egyptian Book of the Dead*, by Chronicle Books. J. Daniel Gunther has lectured extensively worldwide and his works have been translated into multiple languages.

www.jdanielgunther.com

Published Books by J. Daniel Gunther

Initiation in the Aeon of the Child
The Inward Journey - Book I
Published by Ibis Press

The Angel and the Abyss
The Inward Journey - Books II & III
Published by Ibis Press

The Visions of the Pylons
A Magical Record of Exploration in the Starry Abode
Published by Ibis Press

Pythagoras
His Life and Teachings
As Co-editor
Published by Ibis Press

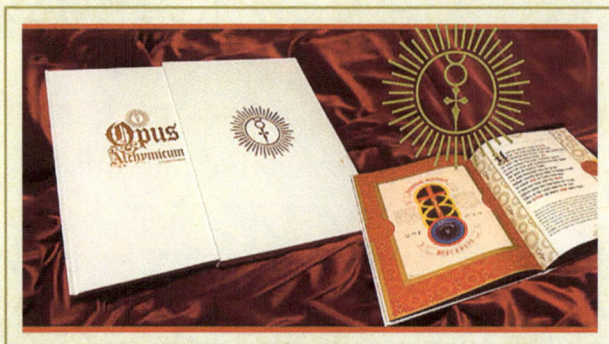

The 2nd Deluxe Edition published by Wennofer House
can be ordered on the author's web page www.jdanielgunther.com

Opus Alchymicum
An Illuminated Epistle on the Stone of the Philosophers
1st Deluxe Edition published by COLLECTIVE 777
2nd Deluxe Edition published by Wennofer House

The Egyptian Book of the Dead
The Complete Papyrus of Ani
Introductory essay, "Coming Forth Into the Day"
20th Anniversary Edition published by Chronicle Books.

Thelemic Lecture Series
An ongoing series of lectures on Thelema
Published by Wennofer House

Parties interested in contacting the A∴A∴ may
address their correspondence to:

Chancellor
BM ANKH
London WC1N 3XX
ENGLAND

www.outercol.org

www.ingramcontent.com/pod-product-compliance
Lightning Source LLC
Chambersburg PA
CBHW061158030426
42337CB00003B/45